W9-BZS-118

Slade Media Center

Abraham Lincoln

By Wil Mara

Consultants
Nanci R. Vargus, Ed.D.
Primary Multiage Teacher
Decatur Township Schools, Indianapolis, Indiana

Katharine A. Kane, Reading Specialist
Former Language Arts Coordinator
San Diego County Office of Education

Children's Press ®
A Division of Scholastic Inc.
New York   Toronto   London   Auckland   Sydney
Mexico City   New Delhi   Hong Kong
Danbury, Connecticut

Designer: Herman Adler Design
Photo Researcher: Caroline Anderson
The photo on the cover shows Abraham Lincoln.

Library of Congress Cataloging-in-Publication Data

Mara, Wil.
  Abraham Lincoln / by Wil Mara.
      p. cm. — (Rookie biographies)
Includes index.
Summary: A brief overview of the life of the man who was President of the United States during the difficult years of the Civil War and who issued the Emancipation Proclamation freeing the slaves.
  ISBN 0-516-22518-9 (lib. bdg.)   0-516-27334-5 (pbk.)
  1. Lincoln, Abraham, 1809-1865—Juvenile literature. 2. Presidents—United States—Biography—Juvenile literature. [1. Lincoln, Abraham, 1809-1865. 2. Presidents.] I. Title. II. Series.
  E457.905 .M32 2002
  973.7'092—dc21

                                    2001008328

People called Abraham Lincoln "Honest Abe" because he believed in doing what was right.

Lincoln was born in Kentucky on February 12, 1809. He grew up on a farm. His family lived in a log cabin.

5

6

Lincoln worked hard on the farm. He also read many books. He loved to learn new things.

Lincoln left home when he was 22 years old. He had many different jobs. He was a storekeeper and postmaster.

9

10

Lincoln wanted to learn about the law. Laws are rules we all have to follow. Lincoln became a lawyer. He also helped make laws for the state of Illinois.

In 1842, Lincoln married Mary Todd. They had four sons.

The Lincoln family lived in Springfield. Springfield is the capital of Illinois.

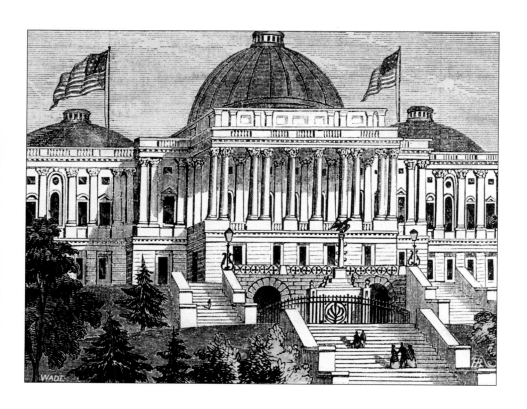

14

Lincoln joined the United States Congress in 1847. Congress makes the laws for the whole country.

The people of the United States believed Lincoln was a very good lawmaker. In 1860, they elected, or chose, him to be their president.

17

18

A war began one year later.
It was called the Civil War.
America's northern states and
southern states fought each other.

At the time, slavery (SLAY-ver-ee) was allowed in the United States. Slavery is when one person owns another person.

21

Lincoln thought slavery was wrong. In 1863, he signed a paper called the Emancipation Proclamation (e-MAN-sih-pay-shun PROCK-luh-may-shun).

This freed all of the slaves.

The Civil War finally ended in 1865. Some people were very angry with Lincoln for freeing the slaves. One of those people was John Wilkes Booth.

26

On April 14, 1865, Lincoln went to see a play with his wife. Booth shot Lincoln inside the theater. Lincoln died the next morning.

"Honest Abe" did what was right, even when others did not agree with him. He helped the United States become a place where everyone could live free.

29

Words You Know

John Wilkes Booth

Civil War

Emancipation Proclamation

lawyer

30

Abraham Lincoln

log cabin

slavery

storekeeper

31

Index

About the Author

Wil Mara has written over fifty books. His works include both fiction and nonfiction for children and adults. He lives with his wife and three daughters in northern New Jersey.

Photo Credits

Photographs © 2002: Archive Photos/Getty Images: 21, 31 bottom left (Hulton Getty Collection), 3, 5, 22, 31 top left, 30 bottom left, 31 top right; Hulton Archive/Getty Images: 29 (Roger Smith), 17, 18, 23, 25, 30 top left, 30 top right; Illinois State Historical Society: 12; North Wind Picture Archives: 6, 13, 14; Superstock, Inc./ The Huntington Library, Art Collections and Botanical Gardens, San Marino, California: cover; The Lincoln Museum, Fort Wayne, IN: 9, 10, 26, 30 bottom right, 31 bottom right.